THIS BOOK

BELONGS TO

....

....

Author's Afterthoughts

With so many books out there to choose from, I want to thank you for choosing this one and taking precious time out of your life to buy and read my work. Readers like you are the reason I take such passion in creating these books.

It is with gratitude and humility that I express how honored I am to become a part of your life and I hope that you take the same pleasure in reading this book as I did in writing it.

Can I ask one small favour? I ask that you write an honest and open review on Amazon of what you thought of the book. This will help other readers make an informed choice on whether to buy this book.

My sincerest thanks.

Table of Contents

Chapter 1
History of Government Contracts

(Part I)

In the modern-day, no form of trade, transaction, or any other mutual exchange of goods and services can occur without a contract. This is the case because a contract provides factual proof for two or more trading parties that the concerned transaction has actually taken place. Based on the ancient Anglo-American common law, contracts or contractual agreements legally bind the trader or any other individual to the deal or transaction.

If the individual chooses to bypass the contract or fails to abide by its instructions, the person is bound to suffer from various legal implications. This is why businessmen and entrepreneurs are advised to study contracts before giving their signatures carefully. Once the party is under contract, they have to fulfill their end of the bargain and meet their responsibilities in a timely manner. Failing in either category will result in a loss of reputation for the person, group, or brand itself. As a result, it is vital for any entrepreneur to pay close attention to the details of each contract they sign and try to uphold their responsibilities at all times. [1]Without a contract or some form of a legal binding document, people simply cannot ensure the safety and security of their goods and services. They need contracts to not only authenticate the transaction but also to make sure that their merchandise reaches the consumer or client.

Businessmen require this guarantee; otherwise, they will not be willing to conduct any type of trade with the other party. This is especially true in the case of government contracts. The federal government requires extremely detailed and comprehensive information regarding the business, its employees, and the product line before they can enter into a contract with the private sector. They carefully analyze each business proposal and only enter into an agreement with those businesses that can provide this Intel in a professional manner. As a result of these prerequisites, the USA government manages to successfully procure more than $300 billion worth of products and items from the private sector each year. These items come under at least 4000 categories and consist of anything from airplanes all the way to t-shirts and household products. Usually, the US government makes its requirement known to the general public by either the local media or through a media service called the Commerce Business Daily.

This particular publication can be found in large public libraries, and through it, the business owner can identify the government's needs and easily enter into a government contract. Unlike most industries, in the case of government contracts, the entrepreneur doesn't have to do prior research and gain awareness on every segment of the industry. All they need to do is visit one of their public libraries and learn about the prevailing government needs and develop the product accordingly.

At the same time, the business professional needs to know that their dealings with the government need to be in an open environment. In order to maintain transparency, the sales of any government contract are performed openly so that the trader or entrepreneur can voice their concerns without any delays or uncertainties. Other than this, government contracts normally involve bulk sales and purchases. As a result, the entrepreneur or businesses professional can double their revenue streams or overall profitability by applying for one or more government contracts. Also, the government contract doesn't expire in a short amount of time. In most cases, government contracts last for more than three months. This gives the entrepreneur an ample amount of time to build a strong relationship with the federal authorities and successfully continue their operations in the imminent future.

In addition to this, the laws and stipulations of government contracts offer the business owner a chance to perfect their operations and meet the standards of the present day. What's more, government authorities have separate approaches based on the type of business that they are dealing with. For example, if the government wishes to trade with small businesses, women-based ventures, and minority-financed companies, the terms and conditions of the government contract will be extremely lenient.

On the contrary, if the local government deals with medium-large organizations, the government contract might have stricter policies and quality standards. In either case, having a government contract allows the entrepreneur or entrepreneur to perfect their operations and effectively deal with any client or consumer. These are the benefits of owning a government contract, and it is vital for brands and organizations to understand government contracts and avail them as much as possible.[2]

If you look at the history of government contracts, one of the reasons behind the interest of federal government towards the private sector rests is their inability to provide input or raw materials for their own services and product line. Since the federal government mostly provides public goods such as defense items and local infrastructure, they are not able to procure quality raw materials for other goods and services.

In most cases, public goods can are non-excludable, so there is no need for the government to maintain its quality for longer durations. This is why, in order to provide optimum quality to the public, the federal government needs the aid of the private sector. The raw materials of certain merit goods, which include education and healthcare, can only be provided by the Private Sector. As a result, the federal government is left with no choice but to engage the private sector and offer government contracts to meet their needs.

Typically, government contracts are offered frequently to manufacturers as they have the capacity to create bulk items and provide them quickly to the government authorities. Once the federal government has signed an agreement with the company, they are legally bound to manufacture and supply the materials as soon as possible. Even if the government manages to procure raw materials on their own, they are never able to cater to the needs of every citizen.

This is why the federal government always turns towards private sector organizations and enters into a contractual agreement for at least two or more years. Once the need is fulfilled, the federal government can either relinquish the government contract or renew it to meet other needs and specifications. In most cases, steel and textile manufacturers are under government contracts as they provide the essential needs for the establishment.

These crucial needs include the development of police cars, military uniforms, vehicles, and school buildings just to name a few. As mentioned previously, the federal government needs to issue a tender in advance in order to remove any doubts, fraud, and uncertainties. There is always a high risk of corruption in government contracts, and because of this, the local or federal government needs to be as transparent as they can.

They need to ensure that the complex procedure of government procurement stays functional for an extended amount of time, and it doesn't fall prey to the hands of decadent politicians and civil servants. Ideally, when issuing the tender, the federal government must include every detail regarding the process, finances, and duration of the contract. By doing this, the government can not only ensure transparency but remove any principal or agent issues that may occur during the procurement process.

The scope of any government extends beyond the reach of any private sector enterprise. And, because of this fact, entrepreneurs need to understand the basics of government contracts and avail them as soon as they occur. The business can profit immensely from one or multiple government contracts, and this is why they need to be on the lookout for any tenders or offerings within their vicinity. Once the business owner has identified the present need of the government, they can start developing the product line immediately. [3]If one wishes to avail government procurement and contracts in the United States, they have to meet certain pre-set criteria.

First and foremost, the entrepreneur needs to understand the process of US government procurement. They must understand which areas the US government covers and how frequently they use the private sector. On a holistic level, government procurement can be defined as the process by which the federal, state and local government bodies in the US procure goods, services (including construction), and certain interests in real property. In the fiscal year of 2016, the US Federal Government managed to spend an excess of over $461B on contracts. At the same time, the usual government contracts for federal procurement largely involve appropriated funds that are then spent on supplies, services, and interests in real property. The federal government carries out this process by the use of purchases or leases. They uses it to procure the supplies, services, or interests which are either already in existence or must be created in the long haul. Then, the US government gives its instructions to get the product developed, demonstrated, and evaluated within a particular time period. The Federal Government contracting process needs the same legal elements as contracting between private parties.

Among these requirements include a lawful purpose, competent contracting parties, an offer, and an acceptance that complies with the terms of the government offer. This offer needs to be under the mutuality of obligation, and consideration of the government and federal authority.

On the other hand, as compared to the private sector, federal procurement is much more heavily regulated because it is subject to volumes of statutes dealing with a number of federal contracts and the federal contracting process. These statutes mostly revolve around the titles of the 10, 31, 40, and 41 of the United States Code. Private parties entering into a contract with one another in the case of commercial contracts have more freedom to establish a broad range of contract terms. They can do this by mutual consent as opposed to a private party entering into a contract with the Federal Government. Every private party represents its own interests and can obligate itself in any lawful and legal manner. Federal Government contracts enable the creation of contract terms by none other than mutual consent of the parties. However, at the same time, many areas addressed by mutual consent in commercial contracts are controlled by law in federal contracts and need the utilization of prescribed provisions and clauses.

In commercial contracting, where one or both parties may be represented by a number of agents. The agent's authority is controlled by the law of agency, and the agent is usually allowed to form a contract only with reference to accepted norms of commercial rationality. And, they are also liable to a few unique statutes that apply in the procedure. In the case of USA Federal Government contracting, the specific regulatory authority is needed for the Government's agent to enter into the contract, and that agent's authority is strictly monitored and regulated by statutes and regulations. The same regulations that reflect national policy choices and prudential limitations on the right of federal employees in order to obligate federal funds accordingly. On the contrary, in commercial contracting, the law enables each side to rely on the significant other's authority to make a binding contract on agreeable terms that are applicable to both parties.

Also, the authority of a Contracting Officer, which is the Government's agent, is to contract on behalf of the Government.

They fulfill this duty through public documents (a warrant) that a person dealing with the Contracting Officer can review at all times. The Contracting Officer does not have the power to act outside of this warrant or to diverge from the laws and regulations controlling the Federal Government contracts as a whole.

As a result, the private contracting party has to be aware of the limitations of the Contracting Officer's overall authority. Even if the Contracting Officer does not know of its duties themselves. In light of this fact, contracting with the United States is a much more structured and restricted procedure than the commercial process for the exchange of goods and services. Once they are aware of these stipulations, the business owner can enter into a US federal contract easily and without any restraints.[4] Apart from contemplating the technical aspects of US government contracts, the business professional needs to be aware of the advantages of government contracts. They need to know how the government contract is impacting their present inflows and then make a decision based on their feasibility. Among the many benefits of government contracts, some of the most well-known advantages include:

The Government Happens To Be The World's Largest Buyer.

The annual contracting marketplace of the US federal government hovers between the $350 billion and $500 billion marks. This makes the U.S. federal government easily the world's largest procurer of products and services. Even if the business professional ignores the contracting opportunities available in the respective industry, they can earn significantly by entering into a government contract. As a matter of fact, they can single-handedly manage all of their expenses by agreeing to a long-term government contract.

Government Contracts Hugely Favor Small Businesses And Enterprises

Based on the $500 billion the U.S. government invests annually on federal contracts, their focus is on <u>allocating 23% of those funds</u> to small businesses and women-owned enterprises. On the surface level, this might sound like a large amount. However, looking at the bidding process and situation, there is no practical guarantee that the federal government might choose one's business. The chances could increase when the individual owns a small firm as compared to a larger institution. On the other hand, in the private industry, the chances of getting a private contract for small businesses are none to slim.

Plus, as a result of the <u>Federal Procurement Data System</u>, the business owner is given the opportunity to identify government agencies that are not meeting or living up to the standard 23% target. If one was to respond to the request for federal proposals or contracts from a government-based agency, the business owner would get preferential treatment over all other non-small or medium-term business firms.

Considerable Intel Regarding Government Contracts

If one was to think about the last proposal or bid they had sent to a prospective customer, along with the time they spent on preparing that bid and setting their rates, they will always arrive at a particular conclusion. They will think how comfortable it would have been to know exactly what the customer was looking for and how much they were prepared to spend on that commodity. If the individual had this answer, it would be a complete game-changer for their brand. While in private sector enterprises this wish may seem farfetched, bidding, and procuring government contracts for a small business can turn this convenience or dream into a reality.

This is the case because federal agencies are required by law to develop written budgets annually, which contain minute details of exactly what they intend to purchase and the funds they have allocated for those purchases. All of these budgets are available in the public domain through none other than the Office of Management and Budget (OMB) website. So, if the business owner is willing to dig in and do some research, they can get the inside Intel on any and all of the prospective consumer's strategies and objectives for the contract and reach an agreement in a swift and easy manner.[5]

(Part II)

Before availing the many benefits of government contracts, we must have a reasonable understanding of the structure of these agreements and why they have become a household name for many businesses. We need to understand the historical background of government contracts and figure out the reasons behind the government's procurement of services, products, and supplies from the private sector.

As we have discussed this before, the federal authorities usually opt for government contracts when they don't have the resources available for certain projects and relief efforts. Every time, the government faces these shortages, they immediately advertise what they need to the general public and private organizations. They send out tenders, issue press releases, and use every media platform to get their point across and complete their projects in a timely and effective manner. Considering their responsibilities, government authorities have to provide welfare to the general public at all costs. They cannot neglect their duties under any circumstances. This fact gives private firms an opportunity to meet the needs of the federal government and gain immensely from government contracts. This norm has prevailed in the USA ever since the signing of the Declaration of Independence in 1776.

As a matter of fact, Robert Morris Jr., a renowned English merchant and the US's first Superintendent of Finance, illustrated the significance of government contracts way back in 1781. During the Revolutionary War, Morris termed government contracting as the *"cheapest, most certain, and consequently the best mode of obtaining those articles which are necessary for the subsistence, covering, clothing and moving of an Army."*

According to Morris, the only way the USA ever stood a chance against the United Kingdom was if they procured as many supplies as they could. Under Morris' tenure, the newly conceived USA went through a long list of reforms. Most of these reforms were based on the laissez-faire principles of Adam Smith. This meant that the USA government at the time had little to no control over its financial contracts, which included military contracts. Under Morris' tutelage, the US government signed its first military contract. The recipient of this contract was based on the sealed bid selection system. The party with the highest bid was awarded the contract, and the military would then receive its supplies and machinery solely from the person or company until the contract matured. Then, after the contract expired, the US government would use the same system and award the new military contract to the highest bidder.

In fact, during this time, Morris even spent his own personal funds and credit to fund the US Revolutionary Army. Morris did this to not only provide the US Military with top of the line equipment and quality materials but also to gain tremendously from his services. And, because of his reforms and contributions, the US government gained a framework for government contracts that lasted approximately 60 years after Morris death.

Based on Morris' vision, the US government and military modified certain elements of the system and adhered to it throughout the early ages of the United States. As a result, all military contracts were conducted, organized, and implemented by private authorities and local citizens of the country. The government, along with the US military itself, had practically no say in the procurement processes. As a result, this system paved the way for wide-scale corruption, fraud, and mismanagement. Private contractors used their authority to conduct fraudulent transactions under false names and credentials. And, because of these deals, the US military didn't receive their supplies and services on time and had to face tremendous casualties. A classic example of these unfortunate turn of events would be none other than the Creek Indian war of General

Andrew Jackson.

On numerous occasions, General Jackson and his troops had to march against the native Indians of Alabama without any food or backup supplies as the sustainment contracts failed to arrive on the scene. The lack of supplies and subpar equipment led to the death of many US troops and had almost sealed the fate of the army. However, fortunately, General Jackson pushed back the Creek Indians and quelled the opposition completely.

The same situation occurred during Henry Atkinson's campaign against the Blackhawk tribes of Illinois and Wisconsin. Atkinson's forces also had to fight most of their battles on an empty stomach and didn't have the weaponry needed to fend off their attackers. In light of these close calls, the US Military was forced to take matters into their own hands. Rather than depending on private contractors, the US Army assigned these contracts to officers within the military.

After the War of 1812, the US army's quartermaster general was put in charge of all military contracts. The official alone would ensure the procurement of each and every military supply, equipment, and machinery. The overall dependency of private contractors and businesses was nearly finished during this time. In addition to this, the performance of capable quartermaster generals, like Brigadier Thomas S. Jesup, showed the US government that it could fulfill its needs efficiently without relying on external sources.

This situation prevailed for a substantial amount of time, and as a result, the USA government was able to save a lot of resources during a number of conflicts. Quartermasters were given a freehand to advertise military contracts, employ the necessary staff in factories and were allowed to conduct small purchases with local merchants and companies. This was why, at the time, the position of quartermaster general was the most sought after position in the US Army. US military officers desperately wanted to become quartermasters and distinguish themselves within the army. For the better half of the 19th century and during the American Civil War, quartermasters performed their duties diligently and provided every need, material, and equipment to the armed forces. Then, before the commencement of World War I, the rapid mobilization of armed personnel and supplies forced the US government to enter into government contracts with private institutions and individuals.

They needed the aid of private bodies to procure and collect a substantial amount of resources so that they could manage the fallout of the First Great War smoothly. Surprisingly enough, these private contractors pulled off their duties in a responsible fashion and didn't commit any serious errors or misdemeanors.

As a result, the US government and military started using private contractors more frequently, and they played an integral role in World War II and other major disputes. In fact, the role of private contractors became so prominent in later years that by the advent of the 21st century, private army contractors faced a staggering 600 percent increase in workload. [6]Judging from these historical developments, we can safely say that government contracts play an integral role in the US federal machinery. Without government contracts, the US government cannot perform its basic functions and secure the welfare of its citizens. Even if the government is able to provide some relief on an individual level, they cannot fulfill each one of their core responsibilities. This is why, over the years, the US government has created several departments to coordinate and facilitate the duties of each and every federal agency.

These departments include the General Services Administration or the GSA, and ever since its inception in 1949, it has become the central agency for managing and coordinating the tasks for every government body within the USA. Apart from this responsibility, the GSA is also in charge of supplying products, raw materials, and other resources to the federal authorities, offering transportation services and office space to federal workers, and the initiation of cost-reduction strategies and policies in the government sector. As a result of these roles and a plethora of other management responsibilities, the GSA consists of 12,000 workers and performs its functions on an operating annual budget of $20.9 billion. This massive budget enables the GSA to supervise and oversee $66 billion worth of procurements each year. In addition to this, the GSA also coordinates and manages approximately $500 million worth of government properties.

These government properties are divided into two groups. The first group consists of 8700 owned and leased buildings while the second group features 215,000 vehicles which are mostly used for motor pools. Out of these buildings, the GSA maintains and manages the illustrious Ronald Reagan Building and International Trade Center (the largest government building in the US after the Pentagon) and the Hart-Dole-Inouye Federal Center.[7] These are just some duties of the GSA, and with the advent of new departments, the authority's responsibilities are expected to double in the near future. Even though the GSA manages and coordinates the federal machinery today, the administration's real mission revolved around the disposal of wartime surplus goods, managing government records, preparing for emergency situations and storing strategic supplies for the US military. However, as time passed, the GSA managed to establish its presence in the public sector and gradually began receiving numerous responsibilities from the federal government. During the 1950s, the GSA successfully performed the overhauling of the White House and went on to gain considerable praise and recognition for its services. The GSA's hard work was appreciated to such an extent that official contractors termed the renovation to be an eloquent restructuring of the entire White House and its associated properties.

The GSA achieved this feat all the while performing its core duties throughout the latter half of the 1950s. Then, in 1960, the GSA created the Federal Telecommunication System. The Federal

Telecommunication System was an intercity service sponsored by the US government that connected every town and city to the national grid. Two years later, the GSA used its Ad Hoc Federal Office committee to send a proposal for new and improved federal office buildings to the US government. The proposal entailed the condition of old and obsolete buildings in Washington, D.C., and provided a solution for this matter. As a result of this proposal, the US government gave the go-ahead for the construction of new and improved office buildings throughout the Capitol. Afterward, during the Nixon Administration, the GSA established the Consumer Product Information Coordinating Center in 1970. This government center was later transformed into the Federal Citizen Information Center, and to this day, it has distributed millions of citizen information publications around the country.

Throughout the 1970s, the GSA successfully initiated multiple plans and programs for the federal government. Among these programs are the Automated Data and Telecommunications Service, GSA Office of Federal Management Policy, the Federal Buildings Fund, and the GSA's Office of Acquisition Policy. All of these government bodies were developed in the years 1972, 1973, 1974, and 1978 respectively, and have completely revolutionized the federal office of information resources. The 1980s were also productive years for the GSA; in fact, in the fall of 1984, the administration introduced the SmartPay program to the US government. The GSA highlighted the ease and efficiency of SmartCards and convinced the government to use these cards for their local transactions. In the present day, the GSA SmartPay program has an excess of 3 million users. One year later, the GSA started taking an active role in the management and procurement of Government Properties by providing the federal government with keen insight on the real estate markets across the country. Then, in the midst of 1987, the GSA set the foundation for its first childcare center in the USA.

Today, the GSA manages 110 childcare facilities spread across each state and facilitates over 8,300 homeless children. The 90s, however, were not exceptionally productive for the GSA as the government agency only initiated two programs in the entire decade. The first initiative was 1994's Design Excellence program (which oversaw the hiring and employment of efficient, responsible, and productive architects for federal construction projects) and the second program was the Courthouse Management Program of 1995 (that paved the way for the largest courthouse building scheme in the USA). These two projects had a profound impact on the citizens of the US, but they were completely overshadowed by the GSA's accomplishments at the turn of the century. The year 2007 witnessed the consolidation of the Federal Telecommunication Service into the Federal Acquisition Service (FAS) in order to meet the ever-growing demand of US citizens and local business. Other than this, in 2009, the GSA created the office of Citizen Services and Innovative Technologies to create a bridge between the citizens and the US government's state of the art IT infrastructure.

These two achievements made a mark in the US public sector and created a positive image of the GSA in the eyes of the government and the general public. Following this, the United States ushered into the 2010s and saw the rapid rise of the GSA and its initiatives. In 2010, the GSA started working on 500 American Recovery and Reinvestment Act (ARRA) projects across the 50 States of America. These projects not only maintained federal buildings, but they upgraded them with modern machinery, new lightings, water-saving gears, and other necessary repairs.

Apart from this, in the same year, the GSA became the first federal body to shift their online communication and email systems to cloud computing software, which reduced discrepancies and federal expenditures by 50%. This was a revolutionary act for any government agency, and because of the GSA, many government bodies changed their systems accordingly. Then, in 2013, the GSA introduced three innovative and groundbreaking programs that enabled the US government to adjust their operations in the digital age.

The first of these renowned programs was the Total Workplace Initiative. As a result of this initiative, federal offices were restructured in order to reduce space, promote collaboration between the public and private sector, and adopt IT-based solutions for the public and federal workers. The second program was called the Presidential Innovation Fellows (PIF) program, and through it, the GSA employed thousands of talented, diverse, and successful IT developers to work on at least 12-month long government projects.

This program was so successful that in January 2017, it was made a part of the US legislature. The third and final program of 2013 was referred to as the 18f, and it attracted a total of 15 web designers, engineers, and product specialists to work on the Federal Government's present digital services and enhance them as much as possible. All of these programs became hallmarks for the GSA, and by 2016, the government body introduced the Acquisition Gateway in order to unite every federal government contractor into a single community.

Much like the rest of GSA's initiatives, this program was also a resounding success, and it set the foundation for two more technology-based government programs. The first program centered on the various companies in the private sector and their facilitation. This program was called Making it Easier (MIE) initiative, and it promoted the government correspondence with prominent IT companies within the country.

The second program was a mixture of the GSA's past and present ventures, and it was referred to as the Technology Transformation Services (TTS). The TTS catered to a variety of government avenues, which included Federal IT solutions, national construction, and the technological education of federal workers and government servants. [8] By using GSA's numerous programs and initiatives, any brand or organization can learn about the federal government's needs, and profit immensely from the opportunity. These brands can reach out to the GSA through any platform and offer their solutions in an impactful and precise manner. Then, upon procuring the government contract, the organization can double its revenue streams in a short span of time and expand their operations both within the country and on the international front.

Chapter 2
Registering your company to do business with your local Municipalities

We have already learned the extensive history of government contracts and have focused on the benefits of government contracts and learned why certain standards and regulations are still being used to this day. Now, in this chapter, we will shed light on the techniques and methods of starting one's own municipal-based businesses. Unlike the standard business licenses given out in the States, doing business with municipalities requires a completely different approach.

This is the case because conducting business with any municipality cannot be authorized in a simple manner. In light of the risks associated with government contracts, no entrepreneur can enter into an agreement without following specific protocols. These protocols need to be followed by the entrepreneur at all times; otherwise, the entrepreneur could face lethal legal ramifications. As a result, the entrepreneur has no choice but to gain awareness regarding these protocols and requirements and adhere to them to the best of their ability. Ideally, the entrepreneur should not leave out any details in their proposal and should have a comprehensive understanding of the specific requirements of the municipality. These requirements could range from supplying raw materials all the way to supervising the inventory of the government. And, in order to complete the registration, the business owner needs to understand these requirements and cater to them systematically.

Many municipalities are responsible for the procurement of supplies for construction and repair work throughout the city.

Municipal officials need these materials at all times; otherwise, they won't be in a position to manage the city or municipality.

As a result, these companies regularly issue contracts for these supplies and avail the services of private contractors. This gives a great opportunity to private businesses and entrepreneurs to procure the government contract and officially commence their operations. In most cases, state or municipality contracts are only awarded to those business professionals who have successfully responded to the Request for Proposal (RFP). The RFP is a document issued by the Division of Purchase and Property, which contains a detailed description of the municipality's needs at the time. If the business is able to provide these needs, then they can apply for an RFP and participate in the auction. However, if the entrepreneur is unable to provide these materials, they will have to wait for the next RFP and apply for it accordingly. All in all, the entrepreneur must fulfill the initial criteria of the municipality; otherwise, their chances of procuring a contract are next to impossible. Other than state contracts, businesses also have the option to enter into a Cooperative Purchasing Program and register themselves into the municipality.

Municipalities have the authority to procure their needs from the public procurement process, and they exercise this right through Cooperative Purchasing Programs. These programs enable the municipality to purchase the state contract without going through the bidding process. Once the municipality has purchased the state contract, they can procure the brand's materials and fulfill their needs in a step-by-step fashion. The Cooperative Purchasing Program is perhaps the most effective tool for local municipalities and is commonly used in the country. There are a number of options available to the municipality as well as the entrepreneur, and based on their feasibility, they can utilize the method accordingly. In the classic method, the municipality procures a material or supply based on the projected cost of the project. This projected cost should not exceed the bid thresholds established by the state; otherwise, there would be no agreement whatsoever.

These bid thresholds are established on a five-year basis, and the municipality can choose to hire a QPA (Qualified Purchasing Agent) or Non-QPA to elevate the bid threshold. However, the thresholds and the legal essentials for each state and municipality may differ. This is why it is imperative for the entrepreneur to be aware of the requirements before embarking on their business journey.[9]

Apart from the needs and methods employed by municipalities, the entrepreneur must also comprehend the licensing needs of the state body or municipality. Moreover, the entrepreneur also needs to understand that their local municipality may require a license depending on the type of business and its location. These two elements are fundamental aspects that need to be defined by the entrepreneur before entering into an agreement with the municipality. Furthermore, if the entrepreneur is establishing a new business venture (which includes home-based businesses), developing a fresh structure, and shifting into an existing structure, then it is vital for the business owner to find out whether the area of operations is zoned for their specific type of brand.

They additionally need to be aware of this fact in order to make sure that they have the right permits or legal authorization to start their business. Other than this, preferably, the business professional must also contract the local municipality and discuss the by-laws, zoning obligations, work permits, and other rules and regulations that could influence the start-up for the brand or business.

Typically, a zoning by-law caters to the utilization of land in one's community or state. The zoning by-laws ultimately determine how the land or property of the business is used, where the business' buildings can be built, parking needs of the business, and other uses of the business' infrastructure. At the same time, it is crucial for the entrepreneur to make sure their use of the property is allowed by the Zoning by-laws. Since nearly every municipality has its own specific zoning, the entrepreneur needs to have detailed maps of the location in order to facilitate their operations. In most cases, businesses operate in three distinct zones. These distinct zones include:

- Office/Commercial
- Retail
- Industrial

Other than these three broad categories, there are also a number of zones that come under the mixed-zone category. A mixed-zone comprises of both business and residential use of the property and can be utilized interchangeably by the entrepreneur. In addition to this, the areas zoned under rural and agricultural categories also come under mixed zones. A classic example of mixed zones would be none other than fruit stands. These fruit stands are authorized in a plethora of municipalities for locations zoned under agricultural. These zones determine the specifications of size, distance from the main road, and other details of the fruit stand while allowing them to conduct their business. If the entrepreneur wishes to change their utilization of the land or property, which is not under the current zoning by-law, the business professional must apply for a zoning change. A quick way to do this is by contacting one's local Municipality's Planning Department. Once the entrepreneur has made the change and contemplated the essentials of zoning by-laws, they need to shift their focus toward building permits. In simple terms, a building permit can be defined as a license for the creation, overhauling, and destruction of any building or structure. If the business is operating on a small-scale, then it is imperative for the entrepreneur to procure a building permit in order to authenticate these actions:

- Developing a new structure within the property of one's business
- Altering the structure of a building
- Fixing or repairing the plumbing system of the RAND
- Installing or revamping the on-site sewage system of the property
- Making considerable changes to the internal boundaries of the building

In order to achieve this permit, the entrepreneur needs to contact their local municipality. It is highly recommended for any entrepreneur to connect with the Building Department and mutually agree on the requirements of the brand, get advice on the legalities, and evaluate the entire application process. After obtaining this permit, the entrepreneur can officially commence their operations with the municipality. However, before obtaining the permit, they need to approve the site plan for their business. A site plan usually consists of a drawing or set of drawings that depict the physical arrangement of the property's alterations.

These alterations include buildings within the property, the driveways, parking locations, pedestrian sidewalks, landscaping, fences or barriers, light fixtures, sanitation, and other municipal services. Site plan approval is essential for the entrepreneur, as without it, one cannot receive a building permit for major renovations, additions, or construction of commercial, industrial or institution infrastructure. This is why it is vital for an entrepreneur to interact with the Planning Department in one's local municipality in order to learn about the site plan of one's project. Upon understanding the site plan, they need to submit the plan for approval to the Planning Department and figure out the approval process. Ideally, the site plan approval process is supposed to be an interactive process, which involves both the property owner and municipal staff. The reason behind this is that these parties need to match the entrepreneur's requirements with both the unique features of every property and the municipal development standards and guidelines of the state. As a result, the approval process facilitates the functional development of the property, all the while minimizing the adverse effects of the uses of the surrounding land.

After getting the approval of the site plan, the entrepreneur must gain awareness of the Business Improvement Areas of the state. From a business standpoint, Business Improvement Areas are locations within a specific town (usually within the downtown area) in which entrepreneurs have to pay an additional tax or fee in order to fund their enhancements to the projects. These enhancements are only allowed within the boundaries set by the BIAs, and they can offer a strategic edge to the brand. Apart from this, BIAs can also provide certain services to the municipality. These services include cleaning the streets, capital improvements, development of streetscape, and marketing the area to the citizens. It is important to note that BIA services are supplemented by the services typically provided by the municipality. Normally, the BIA taxes are part of the property tax bill for any business. After obtaining and understanding these regulations, the entrepreneur can maintain his business relationship with the municipality for a longer period of time. They need to try their level best to improve this relationship and should be aware of the requirements of other governmental institutions. In most cases, when entering the government marketplace, most entrepreneurs wish to conduct their business directly with federal, state, or local government agencies.

Nonetheless, they fail to realize that getting into a contract directly with a government entity involves many steps. In addition to these steps, the brand itself needs to have a established presence in the concerned industry. As a matter of fact, there are a plethora of considerations before the entrepreneur can officially sign a business deal with the government as a prime contractor. Some common considerations include:

- Thorough knowledge of all applicable procurement regulations and laws.

- Being registered in various vendor databases and keeping oneself updated.

- Extended market studies to recognize future tasks and responsibilities.

- The skills needed to evaluate government solicitations and then prepare detailed and responsive offers to the municipality.

- The tact of securing bid, performance, and payment bonds, if needed.

- The financial strength needed to fund a multi-million dollar project for at least 60-90 days before the arrival of the first payment.

- Having strong relationships with different agencies, such as buyers and end-users.

- A healthy track record of relevant experience.

If the business lacks any of these requirements, then it must opt for another business opportunity apart from the municipality and the local government.[10]

The Alternatives to Conducting Business with the Local Municipality

If a business owner desperately wants to procure government contracts despite their limitations, they can avail certain indirect opportunities. In fact, less experienced or smaller businesses can avail a simpler, faster, and less burdensome means to break into the government market.

This straightforward method is none other than subcontracting. When an entrepreneur undergoes the subcontracting route, they can conduct regular business with the government in a completely indirect fashion. They can accomplish this feat through the aid of a prime contractor. The prime contractor can easily handle the smaller pieces of work of the business and can involve fewer requirements than a typical government institution. Additionally, a subcontractor is answerable to the prime contractor and not the government. All the while, the prime contractor bears all the responsibilities as far as the government is concerned, whereas the institution will question them regarding the development of the project. This is why prime contractors have no choice but to fall under government contracting requirements. In addition to this, prime contractors must have the ability to finance the project, maintain the relationship between all parties, and complete the task on schedule. Apart from this, prime contractors are also accountable for catering to any and all socioeconomic small business goals linked with the original contract. In light of these specific requirements, prime contractors are always on the lookout for talented small businesses to meet their needs effectively.

In the case of federal contracts, prime contractors deal with small and medium-term businesses that are managed by women, minorities, disadvantaged groups, and veterans. Other than these types, small businesses situated in historically undermined business zones (HUBZones) are also the primary choice of prime contractors. As a matter of fact, certain individual, state, and local municipalities also have preference programs that deal with small businesses. The key point to note here is that relationships always matter, and having cordial relationships with prime contractors is a NECESSITY. As a result, small firms seeking to enter contracts with large-scale prime contractors need to develop a convincing strategy in order to establish their presence. Through this image, they can inspire bigger firms to award them with numerous projects and develop an impeccable reputation. Moreover, most small businesses in contract with a government prime contractor report that they have received repeat business from their business partners. Therefore, in order to embark on the subcontracting path, the entrepreneur needs to make certain changes in his approach:

1. Have substantial knowledge of the government sector.

2. Find any areas of the government market that are one's forte.

3. Be on the lookout for work areas where the entrepreneur can cater to a specialty requirement or a niche market.

4. Publicize the brand in the government's various small business preference programs and learn how to qualify.

5. Develop and refine a presentation about the business' capabilities and strengths.

6. Communicate one's credentials to prime contractors.[11]

Chapter 3
Registering your Company to do Business within your State

DUNS number

After making the decision to enter into a government contract, the entrepreneur needs to conduct a final task before entering the government sector. This final task is the creation of the government contract proposal in order to receive the bids of the municipality or institution.

Without creating the government contract proposal, the entrepreneur cannot officially commence his business. In order to start receiving bids on government proposals, the entrepreneur needs to get a Dun & Bradstreet (DUNS) number. A DUNS number is simply a unique nine-digit identification code for the physical locations and all associated areas of the brand.

This is an important identification because, without it, the government will never recognize the business as an official partner. In order to register for the DUNS number, one needs to have the following documents:

- The Legal Name of the Business
- The Base of Operations and address of the brand
- The Doing Business As (DBA) document or any other recognizable name of the brand
- The Physical address, city, state, and ZIP Code of the Brand

- Mailing address (if different from the headquarters or base of operations and/or physical address)

- Telephone number

- Contact Name and Title of the Entrepreneurs

- The total number of employees at one's physical location

- Determining the type of business (even if it is home-based)

NAICS Code

Apart from the DNS identification, the brand must also align its products and services with the North American Industry Classification System (NAICS) code. In simple words, the NAICS codes categorize businesses according to the respective product or service they supply for the municipality, local or federal government. Usually, a business has a primary NAICS code. However, it can apply for multiple NAICS codes, if the brand sells more than one type of brand or services. In order to figure out the NAICS code, the entrepreneur needs to view the NAICS code list in the U.S.A. Census Bureau.

However, before obtaining the NAICS code, the brand must fall under the standard illustrated by the NAICS code. An important point to note here is that in order to become eligible for government contracts reserved for small businesses, the brand must also meet the requirements of the size already set by the SBA.

These particular size standards determine the maximum size that a business and its affiliates need to be so that they can qualify for a government contract. The SBA also provides a standard size for each NAICS code. Normally, industrial companies with 500 employees or fewer, along with most non-industrial businesses with average annual receipts coming under the $7.5 million qualify as small businesses for the SBA and NAISC. Yet, still, there are exceptions for certain industries. [12] After registering the brand with the state and acquiring the NAISC and DNS code, the entrepreneur must draft an effective and compelling capability statement. A capability statement is a prerequisite for any government institution or municipality, and they need to be created by the entrepreneur during each business stage.

Aside from the technical and legal requirements of a capability statement, the statement can also be used as a great tool to differentiate one's brand from the rest of the competition. This is the case because a capability statement contains exclusive details of the company and acts as a resume for the local government or municipality.

It can be of use if the entrepreneur is left with no choice but to develop a comprehensive and compelling capability statement and illustrate the brand's qualities in an impeccable manner. In addition to this, the state also uses the capability statement to evaluate one's brand as compared to other players in the industry. Other than the government, a variety of stakeholders connected with one's company also analyze the capability statement and then make their decisions. These influencers or decision-makers include preference program developers, contracting officers, prime contractors, and small business experts. Even the most successful company can portray an unprofessional or amateur demeanor if they have an unstructured capability statement, which could make formatting and structuring crucial to developing an influential capabilities statement. Ideally, a brand's capability statement must be thorough, should not have unnecessary details, and must be readable.

At the same time, the capability statement should not be easy to search and needs to be created using an accessible format, such as a PDF document. Aside from this, in most cases, businesses develop the capability statement either by using Microsoft Word or Publisher. Furthermore, if the entrepreneur already has an established company logo, then they need to incorporate it in the capability statement along with any professional photos that could enhance the brand's reputation. In addition to this, the color scheme used in the capability statement must match with the brand logo. If it doesn't, then it could hinder the entrepreneur's chance to procure a government contract. This is why it is imperative for the entrepreneur to make sure that the marketing materials utilized in the capability statement comply with the organization's branding. In addition, the entrepreneur needs to be aware of the fact that even the smallest details can either improve their chances of securing a government contract or impair their hard work completely. This is why the entrepreneur needs to take care of these three essential elements before completing a capabilities statement:

- Fonts
- The Overall Usage of Bullet Points
- Word Choices or Writing Style

In order to perfect the capability statement's appeal and presentation, the entrepreneur could also choose to employ a graphic designer and/or professional writer. By doing this, the entrepreneur will not only be able to remove the capability statement's mistakes but will also ensure that the statement appeals to the government contracting agency or institution. Preferably, the capability statement must be a flexible document. This means that the capability statement needs to be structured in such a manner that it can be changed easily based on the targeted agency or municipality. The reason why the capability needs to be changeable is that every municipality or government agency has its specific goals and objectives. As a result, it is imperative for the entrepreneur to cater to these goals and missions through the capability statement. Furthermore, the capability statement should not contain any unnecessary information. On the contrary, the entrepreneur must only mention the key details of the brand and tailor it to meet the municipality's expectations. In order to add more value to the capability statement, the entrepreneur must be able to accurately answer these five basic questions:

- Why is the entrepreneur carrying out his business objectives?
- Why should the government agency award the contract to the entrepreneur?
- How can the entrepreneur enhance their current capability statement?
- What are the unique features of the brand that make it stand out in the marketplace?
- Is the entrepreneur withholding necessary information from the government agency or municipality?

By answering these questions beforehand, the entrepreneur will be in a position to create an extensive capability statement and fulfill the agency's requirements effectively. Upon successfully answering these questions, the entrepreneur needs to focus on the content of the capabilities statement. While there are a number of formats and patterns available for capability statements, these four elements need to be present, otherwise, the government agency or municipality will reject the statement altogether. These four elements of factors include:

- About Us/Brand Overview
- Core Competencies of the Company
- Past Performances of the Brand
- Differentiators (Unique features or characteristics of the brand)

- Corporate Data:
    - List of Facilities or locations
    - Organizational data
    - Contact Details
    - Relevant codes such as DUNS, CAGE, NAICS[13]

Once the entrepreneur has integrated these four integral elements in the capability statement, they must not focus on identifying the right opportunities. There are multiple ways to achieve this feat. However, the most common method is by searching for tenders and other contracts on online platforms. The entrepreneur can use firms such as FedBizOpps to identify multiple government or municipal contracts and skim through them accordingly.

On the surface level, searching may seem like a relatively simple process. Although in reality, it can be extremely overwhelming. This is the case because, in the initial search, the entrepreneur is bound to be overburdened by the sheer number of opportunities. In order to prevent this situation, the entrepreneur needs to learn the methods of searching effectively on these websites and pages. Whenever they are conducting a search, the entrepreneur needs to include certain specifications of criteria. These specifications include the vicinity of the government contract, contract type, government agency, and keywords. Furthermore, the entrepreneur can also utilize the advanced search options of these websites and find their ideal government contract. In addition to this, the entrepreneur can carry out their search by using a specific NAICS code and come across a number of government contracts. However, when looking for tenders or other government contractors, it is advisable to conduct a narrow search and then gradually expand it.

Doing so will greatly improve the entrepreneur's chances of

identifying the right opportunity and capitalizing on it accordingly. In their search, the entrepreneur will learn that most government contracts carry detailed solicitations. As a result of the legal ramifications, these solicited documents are comprehensive and illustrate the minute details of the government contract. This is why the entrepreneur has to invest a considerable amount of time understanding each document. They need to be selective; otherwise, they will definitely miss out on lucrative contracts and tenders. Yet still, the entrepreneur must read each document carefully and try to contemplate what services the municipality wants from the company. After selecting one's desired opportunities, the entrepreneur needs to move towards the next step, which is to prepare bids. While performing this step, the entrepreneur needs to comprehend one basic fact. This fact is that the government or municipality is always on the lookout for raw materials and services at the lowest price possible. In light of this fact, the entrepreneur has to prepare a competitive bid; otherwise, it will never be entertained by the municipality.

Despite this fact, the entrepreneur must also keep in mind that the pricing of products and services needs to be kept in such a manner that the transaction becomes profitable for the company. Moreover, they must never enter into a government contract just for the sake of it. Instead, the entrepreneur needs to evaluate the market conditions and come up with a compelling and lucrative bid. Initially, determining the price and bid can be extremely tricky. However, with the passage of time, the entrepreneur will gain enough experience to create a bid that satisfies their own needs and the municipality. After creating the bid, the entrepreneur needs to submit it to the government agency.

They need to go over the instructions and details outlined in the webpage and submit it. However, before the entrepreneur makes this decision, they need to follow the instructions of the solicitation package carefully. They must only submit their bid if they are willing to fulfill each and every requirement. Hence, it is imperative for the entrepreneur to figure out the pricing, financial obligations, and logistic requirements before officially submitting the bid.

After the entrepreneur has made and organized these documents, they can post their bid and wait for the municipality's call. Looking at these requirements, the entrepreneur may find the government procurement process to be fairly complex. However, once the entrepreneur is able to learn the municipality's system inside out, they will be able to contemplate the nitty-gritties and avail the contract. Even if they are having difficulty in the processes, the entrepreneur can consult government websites and remove their ambiguity. Conversely, the entrepreneur can also choose to contract their Small Business Administration (SBA) office. In any case, it is more profitable to procure a government as compared to the private sector. One of the more distinct advantages of working with the government is that the entrepreneur can profit from a number of businesses. This is the case because the municipality or government institution typically purchases goods and services on a monthly basis. As a matter of fact, the municipality also conducts trade during recessionary time periods. In addition to this, through government contracts, the entrepreneur can grow rapidly by making large purchases. These procurements will enable small or medium-sized businesses to expand their operations smoothly.

Aside from this advantage, the entrepreneur can also earn a significant amount from government preference programs. While there a number of programs available in the USA, some common ones include 8(a) Business Development, HUBZone, Service-Disabled Veteran, and women-owned small businesses. All of these programs can give the entrepreneur a competitive edge in the market and allow the entrepreneur to establish their position in the marketplace. The entrepreneur can find all the necessary details of these preference programs from the SBA and local government authorities. One of the advantages of competing for government contracts is that they can be substantial. Through this preference, the brand can grow at a steady pace and make the best of any situation. However, some contracts can burden the entrepreneur's finances or exceed capitalization levels. As an example, we can take the case of small companies that are unable to wait 30 to 60 days to get their invoices paid. Normally, the local government takes this much time to meet their end of the bargain. At the same time, other small businesses do not have access to sufficient working capital to pay the government's purchasing order.

These issues can prevent the entrepreneur from becoming a capable government contractor, and in order to avoid this situation, the entrepreneur needs to gather ample funds before opting for a local government contract. [14] There are many advantages to acquiring local government contracts as the government is willing to spend an excessive amount of money for their procurements. A number of cities, counties, and states have a special preference for local businesses in their procurement options as it allows them to grow the city or state's economy. In fact, 45 states, including the District of Columbia, have procurement policies that are geared toward certain businesses. Some of these businesses include veteran-owned businesses, environmentally sustainable companies, and state-based manufacturers. Also, nearly half of these have a preference for small or medium-sized businesses. All the while, the remaining thirty states have policies focusing on purchasing minority and women-owned enterprises.

A 2014 survey conducted by the National Association of State Purchasing Officials discovered that 19 states have a certification program for small businesses, and the other 32 have a certification or preference program for minority-owned businesses. The report further adds that thirty-seven states have also developed "reciprocal laws." These reciprocal laws instruct public contracting agencies to identify the lowest responsible bidder. Therefore, the focus of each entrepreneur needs to be on developing the lowest most appealing bid and acquiring the contract swiftly. Whenever local municipalities choose to spend their money with small firms, these entrepreneurs are able to develop local supply chains and have an economic multiplier effect.

Many studies have guaranteed the effect of this phenomenon, and one of these is a 2009 research from California State University at Sacramento. As per this study, the State of California managed to generate approximately $4.2 billion in additional economic activity along with securing 26,000 new jobs between the years 2006 and 2007. They did this by contracting with disabled, veteran-owned businesses and city-based small businesses rather than larger companies.

In addition to this, another study from Civic Economics analyzed the situation in Arizona and came across a locally owned office supply company. In this company, a staggering 33.4 percent of profits managed to remain in the local municipality.[15] Judging from these statistics, it is imperative for every aspiring entrepreneur to initially target local government institutions and municipalities and increase their reputation and revenues in a steady, productive, and systematic manner.

Chapter 4
Doing Business with the Federal Government

We have already gained awareness of the key methods of registering a brand with the state government and what components must be catered to by the entrepreneur. Now, we will contemplate one of the most important documents needed for registering with the local government. The reason why this document holds profound importance from a State perspective is directly linked with its inherent structure conditions.

The reason behind this is because whatever content the entrepreneur generates in this specific document will ultimately determine whether they will acquire the government contract or not. Among the many documentations and legal requirements required by the government, some of the most essential items include:

Registering with SAM

The entrepreneur needs to register his brand in the federal government's System for Award Management (SAM) before obtaining a government contract. SAM can be defined as a database that government agencies typically use to search for contractors. By using the SAM database, the entrepreneur will be able to validate his business and prove that it is eligible for government contracts reserved for small businesses. Furthermore, the entrepreneur can also determine whether or not their brand is eligible for contracts under an SBA contracting program for the disadvantaged, women-owned, veteran-owned, small businesses situated in underutilized areas across the country. To sum it up, the brand's SAM profile in SAM serves the purpose of a résumé for the government contract. As a result, developing a profile that is both accurate and appealing is imperative to winning or procuring a government contract.

Invitation for Bid (IFB, IFBs)

An invitation for a bid or IFB is the most basic and easily accessible bid for government contracts in the USA. The IFB is also known as a sealed bid, and it is typically used for contracts over $100,000. This fact makes the IFB extremely competitive, and the only way to secure the contract is by casting the lowest bid.

Request for Quotation (RFQ, RFQs)

The third document needs to be a request for a quotation or RFQ. This is another compliance document that facilitates the trade of goods and services priced lower than $25,000. This document is extremely necessary for small and women-owned businesses; otherwise, they will never have the chance to avail a government contract. In most cases, the bid documents for RFQ are simple and easy to use so that the brand can avail the contract swiftly.[16]

A Request for Information (RFI)

In addition to the three aforementioned documents, the entrepreneur must also carry a request for information (RFI). To put it in simple terms, an RFI can be defined as a document entailing the information of various suppliers in the industry. The RFI is mainly used by the municipality when there are a plethora of suppliers, and there is limited information available in the market. Through the RFI, the government is able to shortlist and engage with those organizations that are fulfilling their needs effectively. An RFI typically includes the following details:

- Table of contents

- Outline and purpose of the RFI
- Description of scope
- Abbreviations and terminology
- Template
- Details of next steps - RFP or RFQ[17]

Request for Proposal (RFP, RFPs) or Request for Tender (RFTs, RFT)

Lastly, the entrepreneur must use accurate, descriptive terms about one's brand so that government officials can easily find them in routine searches. The document is none other than the Request for Proposal (RFP), and every aspiring entrepreneur needs to be well-versed in it. An RFP, unlike the IFB, doesn't need a requirement of over $100,000. On the contrary, an RFP or RFT can be utilized for a government requirement of $25,000 or more. Other than this, the RFP also has a separate structure and criteria as compared to the IFB. In the case of RFP, a supplier of raw materials or services cannot be chosen, simply because they have the lowest price. On the contrary, the RFP is utilized by government agencies to produce the most cost-effective solution dependent on their criteria.

In addition to this, a Request for Proposal (RFP) can be simply defined as a solicitation document that is primarily used in negotiating acquisitions with the government and a private contractor. Through the Request for Proposal, the government can easily communicate their requirements to potential contractors and reach a solution that they both mutually agreed upon.

To the very least, the RFP must clearly define the local government's requirement, the expected terms and conditions that will apply to the concerned contract, the content present in the offeror's original proposal, and (for competitive acquisitions) the latent conditions and criteria for assessing the Request for Proposal. If the RFP cannot accurately describe these elements, it will not be considered as an authentic document. Therefore, in order to ensure the authenticity of the document, the issuer of the RFP must take special precautions before formulating the document. To accomplish this feat, the entrepreneur needs to be aware of certain laws and regulations and draft the RFP accordingly. As an example, we can take the case of *FAR Subpart 15.2 "Solicitation and Receipt of Proposals and Information."* This legislation acts as the main resource for any type of government solicitation and contract, and through it, the entrepreneur can devise their RFP effectively. While there are a variety of sections in the RFP, the proposal MUST contain the following components:

- Section A – Solicitation/Contract Form (which comes under the banner of SF-33)
- Section B – Details of the Supplies and Services along with the Prices and Costs
- Section C – Description, Specifications, and the official Statement of Work
- Section D – Packaging and Marking Strategies
- Section E – Inspection and Acceptance Criteria
- Section F – The Performance and Delivery Specifications
- Section G – Data regarding the Contact Administrations
- Section H – Specific or Unique Contract Requirements
- Section I – The Various Clauses of the Contract
- Section J – A Comprehensive List of Attachments of the Company
- Section K – Numerous Statements of Offeror's, which include requirements and Certifications

- <u>Section L – Official Notice to the Offeror</u>, including conditions and requirements for the government entity.
- <u>Section M – A</u> Detailed Evaluation for the Award (which doesn't apply for soul-source documents)

Other than the aforementioned sections and items, the entrepreneur must also include complimentary documents with their RFP. These complimentary documents will add more flair to the RFP while increasing one's chances of acquiring the government contract. Some of these complementary documents include:

- <u>DD's Form 254</u>
- <u>Work Breakdown Structure (WBS)</u> which need to include the Top 3 Levels
- <u>The RFP or Proposal Compliance Matrix</u>
- <u>A</u> Model of the Contract
- <u>A</u> Detailed list of Government Furnished Equipment (GFE)
- A Library entailing the list of Bidders applying for the said contract

Once the RFP is delivered with these complimentary documents, the entrepreneur will most likely receive the government contract and substantially increase their profitability. They need to understand that certain authorities require these documents to authenticate your business, and without them, there is no way to conclude or authenticate a government deal. For example, the Federal Acquisition Regulation (FAR) cannot validate the proposal without the Department of Defense (DD) Form 254. The DD Form 254 needs to be incorporated in the RFP. The National Industrial Security Operating Manual (NISPOM) section 4-103a also requires the inclusion of the DD Form 254. The NISPOM's memorandum specifies that the government must issue a DD 254 form. This form needs to be present for each Invitation for Bid, Request for Proposal (RFP), or Request for Quote (ROQ).

Judging from this, we can safely say that DD Form 254 ensures the contractor (or a subcontractor) that their security needs are met at all times. In addition, the DD Form 254 describes and explains classification guidance essential to any classified document. Preferably, every government acquisition program must have certain communication in the RFP that deals with the Information Assurance (IA) needs of a particular contractor. As a result, it is just as necessary that the associated person communicates these needs to the offeror or the state government. The RFP should also include the terms of compliance and performance provided by the offeror or the state government.[18] Therefore, the entrepreneur needs to understand how stressful the government's RFP or solicitation truly is and then plan their actions accordingly. Ideally, the entrepreneur should not fall prey to anxiety when drafting the proposal. Instead, they need to consider it to be a crucial task that needs to be completed at all costs. This mindset will enable the entrepreneur to approach the writing process with diligence and professionalism.

All the entrepreneur needs to do is conduct proper research, prepare the proposal, and respond in a clear and effective fashion, while simultaneously aligning the RFP proposal with the state government's expectations and specifying just how their brand is the one-stop solution to their needs and aspirations. Each one of these factors must be catered to accordingly; otherwise, the RFP proposal will not be considered by the local government or the concerned authorities.

Therefore, it is imperative for the entrepreneur to realize that preparation is key. If they require a decent response from their government's RFP or any other procurement request, the entrepreneur must prepare themselves and their team according to the requirements set by the government; otherwise, they would be wasting their time and resources. The fact of the matter is that if the proposal fails to comply with the solicitation requirements, then there is a high chance that it will be viewed as nonresponsive by the local government. As a result, the entrepreneur will be left with no choice but to carefully evaluate the solicitation, along with every other applicable schedule, underlying clauses, and the associated documents.

The case is that the RFP is designed specifically to offer respective bidders with the necessary information needed to draft a successful or productive proposal. The government agency that has offered the solicitation expects every bidder to analyze the document and adhere to it. This is why the entrepreneur must thoroughly review and contemplate the regulations (FAR Parts), which fall under the type of solicitation that the entrepreneur wants to undertake.

It is extremely significant for a brand to come into contact with a contracting officer, PTAC, or other counselors so that they can understand the stipulations of the RFP. In fact, some PTACs and SBDCs even offer designated training on how to develop and submit the brand's proposals. On a fundamental level, proposals or solicitations are normally pretty specific and comply with a standard contract format. The entrepreneur must immediately respond whenever they are contacted by a government agency. In addition, they must answer every question of the government agent, provide extensive information, and stick to the schedules in the required order, time-frame, and structure of the local government. In an ideal scenario, the private contractor must remove every doubt and ambiguity. They can do this by ensuring that their response highlights only that section of the RFP, which the government agency needs and requires.

A clear cut proposal will describe how the bidder can immediately solve the problem or fill the concerned need of the government. However, they cannot achieve this without paying attention to the RFP. It is imperative that the RFP must cater to the government's needs; otherwise, it will stay nonresponsive in the long haul. Let's assume it is bereft of any ambiguity but doesn't cater effectively to the government's requirement; in that case too, it will fall behind those proposals which are geared toward a solution to the agency's issues. In most cases, a government solicitation normally wishes for the bidder to provide immense information regarding their brand and capabilities. Mostly, the government agency relies on capture management in which the contractor must respond to the agency in a swift and detailed manner. Preferably, the entrepreneur must include certain details. He should demonstrate how the firm can effectively fulfill the government's aspirations, why the price they are offering is fair and competitive, ensure that the proposal is well-written, illustrate their previous successes, and lastly, come up with an inspiring story in every part of the proposal.

Moreover, the entrepreneur needs to incorporate this story specifically in the executive summary. By adding the story to the executive summary, it will convince the government agency to recognize the brand's value. It should be taken into account that the brand needs to get its RFP checked by external parties in order to make it as presentable as they can.

Putting aside the technical aspects of the RFP, the entrepreneur must learn from his mistakes in order to bring in the best results. In an ideal scenario, the entrepreneur needs to avoid these certain issues. They should fully comprehend the solicitation and governing regulations of the RFP and must not adhere to a hasty approach. The entrepreneur must never submit an incomplete document, nor should he submit it after the due date has passed. It should be taken into account that the RFP must not lack focus. Additionally, the RFP must not contain any unrealistic pricing, and the entrepreneur should try their level best to avoid any unnecessary errors or complications.

By following these precautions, the entrepreneur will be able to acquire the government contract and profit from it immensely. Even if they are unable to secure the contract, the entrepreneur needs to ask the government agency for a debriefing so they can understand their mistakes and prevent them from repeating. [19] Coming over to the structure of the RFP, this document needs to consist of:

Background

The RFP must contain a comprehensive background regarding the brand so that the local government can easily structure their response. If the entrepreneur has conducted research regarding their target audience, they must include this information as well. The purpose behind this is that the more aware the government is of the target audience and the industry's circumstances, the more accurate they will be able to bring in their early assessment and proposal. Upon detailing the background of the company, the entrepreneur must specify why they are utilizing the RFP. The RFP must comprise pressing matters such as what are the problems that must be solved and why certain strategies have failed? If the brand can clearly answer these questions, the government agency will give them leverage and may even accept their proposal.

Purpose

The next most important element of an RFP is none other than its purpose. It is vital for the entrepreneur to specify the RFP's purpose in a definitive and brief fashion. The entrepreneur must ask themselves whether they want a long-term partner, a vendor to redesign their operations, or they need the government agency for a singular purpose. They must answer these questions in the initial stages so that the government agency can make the right decision. In addition, the business must identify the need for a government contract. In their description, the entrepreneur must point out what they must address and what needs to be omitted from the proposal. They need to include every associated document with the proposal.

Goals

After defining the purpose, the entrepreneur needs to identify their individual goals from the concerned project. They need to highlight why they have undertaken this government contract. There could be multiple reasons, although the business owner must only mention the specific goals. Goals like company awareness, increasing website traffic, doubling sales, are all valid when it comes to issuing the RFP. Furthermore, they must also outline the time frame for accomplishing these goals and how successful they aspire to be. Based on the brand's answers, the government agency will provide their answers accordingly.

Evaluation Criteria

Aside from the goals, the entrepreneur must also grasp the evaluation criteria for the RFP. They need to know how the government is evaluating their proposal and what measures or precautions they must take in order to secure the contract. By doing this, the local government gets an indication of the organization's key values and keeps these values in mind when assessing the RFP or proposal. Therefore, these key points must not be neglected by the entrepreneur.

Wish list

Over here, the entrepreneur needs to specify their wish list items that they will attain from the government contract. If he desires a functionality or deliverable, yet it doesn't fall under their budget, the entrepreneur has the option of securing the government contract and fulfilling their needs. This is why it is crucial for the entrepreneur to present their ideas in a separate wish list section so that every respondent can assess their items and provide a comprehensive review.

Just by addressing these elements, the entrepreneur will eventually construct the RFP and avail the government contract as soon as possible. However, the entrepreneur must also understand one basic fact. On the surface level, there is no pre-set way to construct an RFP. Yet still, if it is not complying with the government standards, the agency will not pay attention to it and reject it altogether. As a result, the entrepreneur must take an ample amount of time to develop an RFP correctly in the initial stages. At the same time, it is preferable to get an opportunity with a government agency that suits one's brand image and vision.[20] Upon incorporating these integral elements, the entrepreneur needs to develop a template for their RFP. Typically, detailed proposals require many writers to complete the process. As a result, these writers produce material with different styles, evident levels of clarity, and immaculate content. If the entrepreneur sends a plethora of templates and writing samples to the writers, then, in that case, they can force them to be on the same page and develop a unilateral document. In most cases, the RFP template should include:

Section Title

Ideally, the section needs to include the summary of the RFP and what the brand hopes to achieve.

Subsection Title

This is a rather simple declarative sentence that defines the main theme of the subtopic.

Understanding

In this particular section, the writer must draft a background paragraph(s), which entails the description and assessment of their customers' needs, wants, issues, and expectations. This section needs to be insightful so that the government agency can make its decisions without any second thoughts.

Solution

This section consists of paragraph(s) outlining the solutions to the aforementioned issues and needs. And, preferably, the writer must draft this section creatively.

Features

In this section, the entrepreneur must shed light on the many features, elements, aspects, and characteristics of the solutions of the previous section. The written material of this section must be extremely clear and concise.

Benefits

This section entails the advantages of the solutions given in the previous section. This section of the RFP must be given extra attention. The entrepreneur needs to be thorough and include evidence of the aforementioned advantages to the consumer.

Conclusion/Summary

In the final section, the entrepreneur must condense the subtopic themes for a second time. However, in this section, the summary should only be of ONE PARAGRAPH.

Writing Guidelines of the RFP

After developing the template, the entrepreneur must instruct his proposal team to adhere to the writing guidelines of an RFP. These guidelines must be followed; otherwise, the chances of rejection will increase by ten folds. Some of these guidelines include:

- The writing style of the RFP is extremely significant as it shows the image of the entrepreneur and the brand. This is why the proposal team must draft the RFP through a logical outline and use topic and subtopic headings to further describe the content.

- After that, the proposal team must structure the first paragraph in such a way that it showcases the primary point before anything else. Ideally, the entrepreneur must review every chapter and topic with a concise paragraph.

- The proposal must not forget to use trigger words to incite attention. These trigger words could be well-known facts, statistics, and explicit reasons to persuade the reader of the main theme. They can use a unique feature, capability, or benefit to highlight the significance of the main theme.

- The document needs to be demonstrative.

- The proposal must include appendices to structure their detailed material.

- The entrepreneur must avoid using unnecessary words or fluff to create an image of the brand

- Also, the entrepreneur must never use subjective adjectives, which can sound boastful to the reader. The proposal needs to be specific and should use particular phrases such as *"10-year track record,"* instead of "excellent track record."

- The proposal team should not use wordy sentences or unnecessary details. On the contrary, they need to conclude their content in a brief and precise manner.

Some common ways of writing clear and concise statements are:

- The content needs to be pragmatically and consistently organized. As an example, we can take the case of a writer outlining requirements, solutions, features of the solution, benefits provided by the solution, and benefits of substantiation, in a specific order. Through this template, every writer has to follow the same pattern.

- In addition to this, the content must also be easy to read and comprehend. A classic way to do this is by including topic sentences, small paragraphs, and no unnecessary or detailed words. Again, the proposal team must use declarative sentences to prove their point.

In the end, the entrepreneur must develop a technical proposal, which is short and unambiguous. By doing this, the proposal team will be able to present the major components of the RFP and make the job of the evaluators (who have to read extensive documents daily) relatively easy.[21] By including these specifications and reviewing the RFP concisely and consistently, the entrepreneur will inevitably secure the government contract and increase their brand's reputation by ten folds. Through the RFP, the entrepreneur will be able to stand out among its competition and earn significantly from the government exploits.

Chapter 5
RFP- Request Proposals, Bids, & Contracts

Similar to grasping and applying for RFPs, Bids, and other documents, it is imperative for the entrepreneur to secure a stable and extensive line of credit. This is mainly because, without a line of credit, the entrepreneur won't be able to fund the requirements and perquisites of the government contract. This case is specifically true in small businesses as these brands have a difficult time gaining the necessary funds. There are well over 28.8 million small businesses operating in the U.S. based on the latest figures revealed by the SBA.

This is a huge number, and each one of these businesses will need a line of credit at one stage of the business. Much like personal credit, business credit ultimately determines whether or not small businesses can be trusted regarding their money management. If the entrepreneur is able to meet his financial obligations in a timely manner, they will have a better chance of securing a government contract. The government agency or department will realize that the entrepreneur fulfills their commitments and might even prefer them in the next bidding session. This is why the entrepreneur must consider their business credit report as a tool to measure the brand's financial reputation and improve on it as much as possible. Once the entrepreneur has perfected his business credit report, he will increase his brand's image by tenfolds and inevitably secure the government contract. However, if the entrepreneur isn't able to comprehend the significance of business credit, they will never receive the funds and may have to terminate their bid in the long haul. Aside from the financing needs of the government contracts, the latest survey confirms that the line of credit is essential to the success of small businesses. Some of these surveys include:

1.

A survey conducted by the NSBA revealed that 27% of businesses were not able to receive the funding they needed to commence their business journey. Other than this, those 1-in-4 businesses weren't able to expand their operations simply because they didn't receive a line of credit.

2.

In addition to this, a study conducted by MasterCard® claimed that 46% of all small businesses utilized personal credit cards in America. This study further added that small businesses continuously fail at separating their business and personal expenses.

3.

Another case study by NSBA Small Business Access to Capital pointed out that nearly 20% of small business loans are denied by banks and loaning authorities. The study clarified that this was mainly because of the businesses' business credit.

4.

As per the research conducted by Creditera, during the initial six months of 2013, both Dun & Bradstreet and Equifax Commercial received 45 million and 35 million business credit report requests, respectively. These top agencies received requests from numerous small businesses across the country and were able to approve only a fraction of them.

5.

Apart from Creditera, the Nav American Dream Gap Survey of 2015 discovered that 45% of small business owners did not even know that they had a business credit score. All the while, 72% were not aware of the destination through which they could find information on their business credit score. In addition to this, 82% of entrepreneurs were not able to interpret their credit scores.

6.

Similarly, a research carried out by Small Business by Demand Media in 2015 determined that the average lender considers a business credit score of 75 as "acceptable" for sanctioning a line of credit. This acceptance rate makes it extremely difficult for small businesses and other companies with lower scores to acquire loans for their operations.

7.

According to Cardhub 2015, a typical small business needs at least 12-18 months to enhance their present business credit score.

8.

In a recent study, Bolt Insurance confirmed that only one in three small business owners borrow money from their immediate family and friends. All the while, 75 percent of small business funds come directly from bank loans and business credit.

9.

A research performed by Mercator Advisory Group claims that small business credit cards account for $430 billion in spending. This implies that almost $1 in every $6 is spent on these credit cards in order to acquire stable credit.

Judging from these statistics, we can clearly see that business credit holds the lifeline for any business venture. Business credit allows the entrepreneur to procure the capital needed to expand their operations, meet day to day expenses, buy inventory, and hire additional staff. Furthermore, business credit also enables the entrepreneur to protect his cash on hand and pay his cost of conducting business.[22] This case applies in the case of government contracts as well. And, because of this, the entrepreneur needs to evaluate the business credit options available to them and then make their decision.

They need to understand that bidding for government contracts can be an effective way to grow a small business. This is mainly because government agencies at the federal, state, county, and city level normally purchase every type of good and service. If the entrepreneur sells a product or service, there is a high chance that the government procures the item if it suits their present needs. Moreover, the entrepreneur must know that government agencies have mandates *to work with small businesses*. As a result, these mandates ultimately level the playing field, so to speak. In addition, these mandates develop a great opportunity for companies that wish to learn how to operate in this specific marketplace. The entrepreneur should be aware that finding a government contract is, in fact, the easy part of the engagement process; however, normally, the fulfillment and delivery of the contract is the area where small businesses mostly experience problems in fulfilling their end of the bargain. These problems usually spring up because very few brands have the necessary funds to complete their government contracts. This lack of funding inevitably puts them in a position to *fail* and default on the contract.

Common financial problems

There is no doubting the fact that procuring a government contract can definitely create financial problems in the imminent future. However, it is also true that even small government contracts can result in higher profitability for small businesses. In most cases, the government's financial demands can drain the entrepreneur's resources. Unless the entrepreneur is mentally prepared for these demands, they are bound to face a lot of cash flow problems. Out of these issues, the two most common problems are:

Problem 1: Slow payments

More often than not, government agencies and departments pay their invoices on an average of 30 to 60 days. However, only a handful of entrepreneurs are aware of this fact when bidding for large government contracts. Ultimately, this payment delay can have serious implications for small businesses. This is why the business must be in a position to meet the expenses associated with the government contract. In addition to this, the entrepreneur must be able to wait 4 to 8 weeks for the payment. This wait can be next to impossible if the entrepreneur has already hired additional staff or if the company does not have a cash reserve. This scenario could leave the entrepreneur unable to pay their employees or suppliers on time.

Problem 2: Not having enough funds to Pay Vendors

Aside from slow payments, the entrepreneur could also face an issue in paying off their vendors. This is mainly due to the fact that usually small product re-sellers and wholesalers have to *prepay* their suppliers whenever they make a purchase. As a result, if the entrepreneur doesn't have the money to prepay the vendors, they will never procure their goods and items. Hence, the entrepreneur, in the long run, would not be able to meet the government purchase order.

Receiving Financing before bidding

If the entrepreneur needs financing, it is best that they acquire it *before they submit their bid*. As a whole, receiving funding can take anywhere from a few weeks all the way to a couple of months. This is why having this resource before submitting the bid can aid the entrepreneur in preventing potential delivery problems in the future. Preferably, the entrepreneur must avoid that situation where they have already won a bid but do not have the funding needed to execute it.

One particular logistical advantage of receiving funding *before* bidding is that it makes financing the project much easier for the entrepreneur. In most cases, the government contract finance solutions depending on the assignment of claims act for payments. Hence, setting the proper assignment when the entrepreneur first submits the bid is quite easy. Contrarily, altering the proceeds assignment way after the bid is submitted could prove to be a time-consuming process. This is the case because it depends entirely on the specific contracting officer.

Government contract financing

While there are numerous methods of procuring a line of credit, there are a total of five commonly utilized solutions for financing government orders. These five solutions are relatively easier to procure than conventional financing. At the same time, these methods can be adopted by small businesses. Moreover, the vast majority of these options are extremely flexible and are ideal for growing government contractors.

Option 1: The Small Business Administration

One of the most effective techniques for financing government projects is to adopt financial solutions provided by the Small Business Administration (SBA). In reality, the SBA provides a plethora of financial products that can significantly aid small and midsize companies. The businesses that require minimal lines of credit should consider Microloans. These lines reach a maximum of $50,000; however, these limits vary from state to state. These microloans are relatively easier to receive as compared to regular bank loans. In addition to this, they are perfect for those entrepreneurs who are just beginning their business journey. Large businesses can opt for CAPLines. CAPLines are a unique brand of 7(a) loan. Furthermore, CAPlines can range up to five million dollars and can be structured in various ways. It is important to note that the SBA does not lend money directly. Other than that, the authority offers guarantees to banks that are willing to underwrite the loans.

Option 2: Invoice financing / AR factoring

Besides SBA, accounts receivable factoring can also eliminate the cash flow problems, especially when these problems arise from slow-paying invoices. An invoice factoring program is a program that deals specifically with government receivables. And, through it, the entrepreneur can easily finance invoices and provide the cash flow needed to pay for operating expenses. Another benefit of factoring is the program's flexibility. This line of credit can grow significantly as the brand's revenues from government projects increase. Qualifying for a factoring program is pretty simple, especially in the case of government contractors. As a matter of fact, setting up the line of credit only takes a week or two. This timeline makes factoring a preferred option for government contractors.

Option 3: Buy order financing

The entrepreneur could also buy order financing. Order financing can aid wholesalers who have large purchase orders and need immediate funding to pay off their suppliers. A PO financing program enables the entrepreneur to meet the supplier costs related to a particular government purchase order. At the same time, this funding allows the brand to fulfill the order and book the revenue. This line of credit is also flexible and is designed especially to facilitate growing orders. However, purchasing order finance can only work for suppliers *who resell products*. Sadly, this business credit can't be utilized by manufacturing companies. Furthermore, this financing solution benefits those government orders that have higher profit margins. Typically, these profit margins are well above 20%. Procuring this line of credit is also simple and requires only a few weeks.

Option 4: Supplier-based financing

Other than this, supplier financing can be an impeccable option for small and midsize manufacturing companies. In addition to this, even product distributors that have government purchase orders and need to pay suppliers can utilize supplier financing. This line of credit is a type of supply chain financing in which the finance company provides credit to the brand and mediates the entrepreneur's supplier purchases. This business credit works only for businesses that have a established track record and have at least three years of operational history. A major benefit of supplier financing is that it fits appropriately with the brand's existing financing. When used appropriately, business credit can expand the entrepreneur's capabilities and enable them to fulfill more orders or create inventory.

Option 5: Asset-based lending

This particular line of credit is designed particularly for larger or more established companies. Large brands that need immediate funding need to consider asset-based lending. These lines of credit allow the entrepreneur to finance the brand's main assets. These assets include the likes of accounts receivable, inventory, along with equipment. In addition to this, asset-based financing can be structured in such a way that they seem like ordinary lines of credit or term loans. However, it all depends on the underlying asset that is being financed in the first place. Moreover, asset-based loans are utilized by growing companies with established financial controls but who seem to never qualify for conventional lines of credit. All in all, this financing solution is available to companies generating a minimum of at least $1,000,000 of total monthly revenues.[23]

The entrepreneur can choose from any one of these business credit options and embark on their contracting journey. All they need to do is assess their feasibility and evaluate their credit report before selecting these financing options. These analyses will help the entrepreneur in understanding their business from the inside out and enable them to make the right financial decisions. After the entrepreneur has selected their line of credit, they need to fulfill the remaining conditions of the government contract and wait for the agency's decision.

Chapter 6
Best Strategies to Win Government Bid, Proposals and Contracts

After understanding the laws and the overall structure of the Request for proposal, we will now turn our attention towards the techniques needed to acquire a government contract in the quickest way possible. These techniques and methods need to be understood by the entrepreneur; otherwise, their proposal may never get accepted by the government.

This is the case because, without these methods, the government or any other associated institution will not take the proposal seriously. Therefore, it is imperative for the entrepreneur to comprehend certain techniques and follow them as diligently as they can. The entrepreneur should only make strategies that comply with these techniques. This will save them a considerable amount of time and resources and guarantee their approval. These techniques can also be divided into a number of steps so that the entrepreneur can adhere to them systematically. After the entrepreneur or business owner has made the proposal structure from scratch, they can enhance their proposals even further by applying a few simple tips. These simple steps are bound to give impeccable results. However, before the entrepreneur can arrive at this outcome, they must adjust their proposal based on the trends or situations. Some of the methods include:

Sending the brand's proposals in the nick of time

It is a proven fact that timing plays an important role in the government sector. If the entrepreneur, by chance, misses any meeting with the government official or team, the likelihood of the brand receiving the government proposal drops significantly. In addition to this, by sending the business' proposals at the right moment, the entrepreneur will definitely be able to reach and compel the highest possible number of recipients.

As a matter of fact, sending a timely proposal is by far one of the easiest ways to boost their open rate. Although in order to attain the full benefits of this technique, the small business owner needs to abide by a few stipulations to this strategy. This is the case because, in reality, the best time to send varies depending on the industry in question. This is why the only way to accurately determine the best time for the business' proposal is by running consistent and regular tests. In order to achieve this feat, the small business owner can utilize a proposal software. This particular software typically consists of tracking tools that enable the entrepreneur to run a plethora of different experiments. That being said, a study conducted by CoSchedule points out that Tuesday at 10 AM is the most efficient time to send any professional email. This email could range from a simple job application all the way to a government proposal. At the same time, in order to send a follow-up email, the coming

Thursday is the best day to achieve a beneficial result. Aside from this, if the small business owner wishes to conduct another follow-up, then the third round should be carried out on a Wednesday. Nine times out of ten, these techniques will aid the small business in securing the government contract. And, by utilizing this information, the entrepreneur can come up with a starting point for their proposal strategy. Ideally, it is better for the entrepreneur to submit their proposal before the deadline.

Operating electronic proposals and signature software

Other than following a timeline, one of the easier methods to streamline the brand's entire proposal workflow is through taking advantage of e-proposal and e-signature software. In most cases, proposal tools and software consist of collaboration and automation functionalities. These functionalities will help the employees and even the entrepreneur himself to significantly cut down the average time needed to develop a proposal. Furthermore, the original drafters of the proposal can benefit from an organized content library and add tested and pre-approved marketing content and legal clauses to the government proposal in a swift manner.

Also, just by using the elements of government proposals which worked in the past, the chances of acceptance can increase dramatically. In addition to this, the proposal software removes the burden of adding electronic signature fields. Moreover, the entrepreneur can run experiments to generate immaculate content and can thereby adjust their follow-up strategy to reach the government institution at the precise moment.

Incorporating templates and track results within the Government Proposal

Certain templates of the government proposal are excellent for one simple reason. This reason is that these templates enable the entrepreneur to copy successful factors from prior proposals and include them in their past performance. This quick and easy technique can save the entrepreneur a considerable amount of time. Furthermore, these templates can easily remove the shortcomings of the writer as well as those of the entrepreneur. This is the case because, even if the entrepreneur excels in marketing the brand, they may not necessarily be efficient or natural proposal writers. This is why, by offering them with the correct structure and precise guidelines regarding the proposal, the entrepreneur can secure quality and professionalism. They can do this even if the proposal drafter lacks writing expertise or experience.

Utilizing rich media like charts, videos, and images

Another impeccable technique for securing government contracts is including rich media in the brand's proposal and additional documents. According to a study, rich media, which includes charts, images, and videos, substantially increases proposal conversion rates by more than 32%. However, in order to achieve these results, there is one crucial point to keep in mind. This vital point may be shown as less worthy, but typically it is more in the scope of visual elements. This is the case because incorporating a plethora of media options can make the proposal complex and difficult to understand. This is why the safest option is to include one or two graphs and images that are essential to the brand's vision. At the same time, the small entrepreneur MUST include pictures of their employees in their company bio.

Theming the proposal in a customer-centric fashion

Besides the theatrical aspect of the proposal, the entrepreneur must be ready to offer additional services to the government agency. These additional services or products must be aligned with the government's values, preferences, pain points, doubts, and other requirements. This is why it is imperative for the entrepreneur to keep these products in mind whenever they are developing their proposals. In order to achieve the best results, each and every section of the government contract proposal needs to be written based on the government agency's requirements. As an example, we can take the case of the bios of team members. These bios normally reflect the relevant experience and case studies of the team. In order to personalize this section, the entrepreneur can carefully select the bios and only include those employees which appeal to the concerned government sector. The information regarding government organizations is available online.

And, because of this facility, the entire research process becomes relatively easy. Additionally, the entrepreneur could attend events and committee sessions in-person. However, it is fairly easy to get lost in all the advice about drafting the right proposals. In this scenario, both large and small brands usually find it difficult to screen, organize, and integrate each and every tip and tactic present on the web. In order to avoid this confusion, the entrepreneur needs to evaluate those companies that have repeatedly won new contracts through their proposals. This direction will turn the process into a well-researched, tested, and efficient system. Just by doing this, the entrepreneur will be able to position themselves well above their competitors and empower their strategies significantly.[24]

Submitting the Questions and Proposals

Apart from theming the proposal, the entrepreneur needs to have a constant flow of innovative business ideas and concepts, which are usually found in government agencies. In most cases, the government is designed to support its citizens on any level. At the same time, the government isn't tasked with or tracked by its innovative practices or solutions.

The entrepreneur can fill this gap by delivering fresh energy, innovative perspectives, and providing relevant solutions. All they need to do is submit groundbreaking questions and their answers in the initial proposal. After doing this, the entrepreneur's innovative ideas, particularly those that have already worked in the private sector, will aid the brand in standing out amongst the competition and securing the government contract indefinitely.

Selling High-Quality Products

Since the government is interested in high-quality work that fulfills a specific need, it is only sensible to convince them of the *genius factor*. The genius factor is none other than things that the brand does exceptionally well. More often than not, small businesses can feel like underdogs or be marginalized when it comes to competing against larger organizations. Yet still, the entrepreneur MUST NEVER underestimate their unique selling proposition (USP) and utilize it as much as possible. The brand's solution may, in fact, prove to be more agile, efficient, and responsive in delivery. The case being that the entrepreneur doesn't have to deal with the bureaucracy found in larger organizations.

Contemplating the Customer

Thus far, the most effective strategy in securing any contract or business has to be none other than discovering the customer's needs and delivering them. While this may seem simple on the surface, it becomes extremely difficult for contractors to grasp and consistently execute these activities. The entrepreneur should always try to address the customer (government) problems first and then offer their solutions. As a matter of fact, the entrepreneur should remember that the solution is always more critical than their problem. They need to realize that winning contractors only secures the contract when they have mastered the art and discipline of customer focus. Moreover, clarifying the government's needs and providing them with impromptu remedies will inevitably alleviate the agency's pain points and will make the brand an official contractor of the government.

Not evading the Process

The entrepreneur must adhere strictly to the government process and should never try to avoid it under any circumstances. Even if they have certain reservations regarding the process, they must submit their inquiries to the government agency. They need to be aware that there is no progress outside of the stated process. Hence, if the entrepreneur wants to conduct business directly with the U.S. Government, the company must first be registered with the Central Contractor Registration (CCR) database. The CCR database gives the entrepreneur a real-time view of how many competitors are present in their industry. At the same time, they can figure out how many rival brands already conduct their business with the government. There are a plethora of government contracts out there. Although, the process in itself isn't always straightforward and should be followed in an articulate manner.

Innovate Through Collectivity

The entrepreneur must know that relationships are essential to government contracting. This case is applicable to government procurement officers. Some government agencies have designated liaisons who will lobby on the entrepreneur's behalf. At the same time, forming partnerships with other small contractors are also critical to the brand's success.

As a result, bidding for contracts by being a part of a team is another great strategy to win more contracts in a short period of time. This is why the entrepreneur must team up with an experienced prime contractor or enter into a bid with another small business. By doing so, he will be able to learn the system and establish an impeccable track record. This track record will help the brand in winning the next contract faster and with lesser resources. Only when the brand has amassed some quality performances will they be in a position to swiftly target agencies as a prime contractor.

Leveraging Current Successes

In most circumstances, entrepreneurs do not invest their time and resources to learn, understand, and adapt to the recent trends. This lack of information can dramatically decrease their chances and opportunities of winning government contracts. As a result, it is crucial for the entrepreneur to research and study other **successful** government contractors.

Especially, those contractors that offer similar services to their company. In addition, the entrepreneur must gain awareness regarding the contract vehicles and corporate certifications that are present in the industry. Following this, the entrepreneur should identify whether or not the target agencies utilize these concerned vehicles or corporate certifications. If they do use these items, then the entrepreneur should avail them at all costs. This single act will enable them to win more contracts in the distant future. [25]

Meeting the Government's Offer

The entrepreneur must be aware of the fact that they can't possibly sell every product in their portfolio. This is why it is vital for the small business owner to go through their inventory and figure out which offer makes the most sense. After doing this, the small business owner needs to conduct research regarding a number of government agencies. By performing this action, the entrepreneur will be able to identify what product line would be a good fit for the government agency.

The more specific the product is, the fewer agencies the brand owner has to pitch. This will work to their advantage if the brand owner is smart enough to select the right approach. In addition to this, knowing the particular needs of the government agency that the brand wants to work with will enable the entrepreneur to solve their issues more efficiently. However, he needs to adjust their standard options so that they can easily match the government's requirements. Due to which, the entrepreneur has no choice but to be as flexible as they can be. Furthermore, the entrepreneur should also be forward-thinking in order to present the brand in a more compelling light. In addition to this, the entrepreneur needs to specify why their product line will satisfy the government institution's needs effectively. While simultaneously, he should also mention in the proposal how the product line can streamline the entire approval. By doing this, the entrepreneur can significantly improve their chances of approval and gain significantly from the government contract.

Consulting a PCR or the Contracting Officer and Getting Listed Accordingly

In order to solidify the brand's chances, the entrepreneur needs to visit a procurement center representative. This procurement officer needs to work for the government agency the entrepreneur wants to work with. This representative performs his duties by acting as a liaison between the entrepreneur and the federal government. In other words, the representative will ensure that the entrepreneur has all the necessary information regarding the bid proposal. The contracting officer or the PCR has a huge part to play in the acceptance process. And, because of this, the entrepreneur needs to establish a harmonious relationship with the contracting officer. Moreover, the entrepreneur must contemplate the fact that each agency will have its own particular bid boards listed on their respective procurement websites. After the entrepreneur has comprehended the bidding requirements needed to win government contracts, they need to get their brand listed in the System for Award Management (SAM).

This specific database operates like a LinkedIn for government contracts. As a result, the entrepreneur must update their business information on a quarterly basis. By doing this, the entrepreneur can keep the government aware of what they are doing and offering to the agency. The more accurate this listing is, the better chance the brand has of winning a lucrative contract from the government.[26] By applying these techniques, the entrepreneur can secure the government with relative ease and embark on a journey of consistent profitability. All they need to do is pay close attention to their proposal and additional documents while amplifying their qualities as much as possible. Once the entrepreneur has successfully strengthened his proposal and included the additional details and specifications of their product line, he will eventually be selected by the government body and become an official contractor.

[1]Contract Law (2018), Contracts, and other Agreements. Retrieved from
https://lawhandbook.sa.gov.au/ch10s02.php

[2] Entrepreneur Asia Pacific (2019), Government Contracts. Retrieved from
https://www.entrepreneur.com/encyclopedia/government-contracts

[3]Stigiltz (2000), Economics of the Public Sector. Retrieved from
https://www.worldcat.org/title/economics-of-the-public-sector/oclc/39485400

[4] ScaleUp USA (2017), How to start a federal contracting business. Retrieved from
https://www.scaleupusa.xyz/courses/How-to-start-a-federal-contracting-business

[5] Wood (2018), Government Contracts for Small Businesses: Where and How to Get
Them. Retrieved from https://www.fundera.com/blog/government-contracts-for-small-
business

[6] Weitzel (2011), History of Army Contracting. Retrieved from
https://www.army.mil/article/54337/history_of_army_contracting

[7] U.S. General Services Administration (2019), The Functions of the GSA. Retrieved from
https://www.gsaig.gov/?LinkServID=908FFF8C-B323-14AD-
270C38936310AEBD&showMeta=0

[8]GSA (2019), A Brief History of GSA. Retrieved from https://www.gsa.gov/about-
us/background-history/a-brief-history-of-gsa

[9] NJLM (2019), Doing Business with Municipalities: What Vendors Need to Know.
Retrieved from https://www.njlm.org/overview_purchasing

[10] Enterprise Centre (2019), Municipal Business License. Retrieved from
http://enterprisecentre.ca/starting-a-business/registration-licensing/municipal-business-
license/

[11] GeorgiaTech (2012), Subcontracting could be your starting point into the government
market. Retrieved from https://gtpac.org/2012/01/09/subcontracting-could-be-your-starting-
point-into-the-government-market/

[12]SBA (2019), Basic Requirements for Government Contract Proposal. Retrieved from
https://www.sba.gov/federal-contracting/contracting-guide/basic-requirements

[13]USFCR (2019), Writing Winning Capabilities Statements in 2019. Retrieved from
https://uscontractorregistration.com/capabilities-statement/

[14] Diego (2019), How to Find Government Contracts? Retrieved from
https://www.comcapfactoring.com/blog/how-to-get-government-contracts/

[15]Mitchell and LaVecchia (2015), Local Purchasing Preferences. Retrieved from https://ilsr.org/rule/local-purchasing-preferences/

[16] James (2019), Government Contracting Terminologies. Retrieved from https://www.findrfp.com/Government-Contracting/Gov-Contract-Term.aspx

[17] PPC (2018), Choosing RFI RFP RFQ as a Sourcing Tool. Retrieved from https://www.purchasing-procurement-center.com/rfi-rfp-rfq.html

[18] AcqNotes (2019), Proposal Development: Request for Proposal (RFP). Retrieved from http://acqnotes.com/acqnote/tasks/request-for-proposalproposal-development

[19] SBA (2014), How to Prepare Government Contract Proposals. Retrieved from https://www.sba.gov/sites/default/files/2018-02/proposals_workbook.pdf

[20] Harless (2015), Writing a Better RFP Starts with Clarity. Retrieved from https://www.forbes.com/sites/theyec/2015/06/04/writing-a-better-rfp-starts-with-clarity/#6b43c0d14038

[21] Fedmarket (2019), Proposal Writing for Government Contracting. Retrieved from https://www.fedmarket.com/contractors/Proposal-Writing-for-Government-Contracting

[22] Carbajo (2017), 10 Stats that Explain Why Business Credit is Important for Small Business. Retrieved from https://www.sba.gov/blog/10-stats-explain-why-business-credit-important-small-business

[23]Gerald (2019), Five Ways to Finance a Government Contract. Retrieved from https://www.comcapfactoring.com/blog/financing-government-procurement-contracts/

[24]Fagan (2019), How to Write a Government Proposal (+5 Tips to Make Yours Better). Retrieved from https://learn.g2.com/government-contract-proposal

[25] Carmody (2018), 6 Steps to Win More Government Contracts. Retrieved from https://www.inc.com/bill-carmody/6-steps-to-win-more-government-contracts.html

[26] Ferriere (2018), How can Small Companies Win Government Contracts. Retrieved from https://tenderspage.com/how-small-companies-can-win-government-contracts/

www.ingramcontent.com/pod-product-compliance
Lightning Source LLC
Chambersburg PA
CBHW080923240526
45472CB00027B/2211